#ME TOO, ANCH'IO

#Me Too, Anch'io

Writings by Italian American Women

EDITED WITH A FOREWORD BY

Daniela Gioseffi

POETS WEAR PRADA • Hoboken, New Jersey

#Me Too, Anch'io

Poets Wear Prada
533 Bloomfield Street, Second Floor
Hoboken, New Jersey 07030
http://pwpbooks.blogspot.com

First North American Publication 2020
First Mass Market Paperback Edition 2020

ISBN-13: 978-1-946116-08-6
ISBN-10: 1-946116-08-4

Library of Congress Control Number: 2019941443

Printed in the U.S.A.

*For my sisters everywhere, particularly my
Italian American sisters, and to all women who
have suffered, or are suffering, sexual abuse,
harassment, and gender discrimination.
May our sufferings end and may we find new days
of peace and solidarity in gender equality.*

Table of Contents

Editor's Foreword

Until I was fifty years old, I never confessed to anyone, not my parents, sisters, husband, daughter or close friends, what constituted the worst moment of my life — rape by a Ku Klux Klansman masquerading as Assistant Deputy Sheriff of Montgomery County, Alabama. At twenty, I was attractive, stylish, ambitious, and serving as an intern journalist on WSLA-TV in Selma, Alabama, away from my home in New Jersey, on leave from Montclair State University, the summer after my freshman year. Wanting to be the next respected television spokeswoman, another Faye Emerson (the Oprah Winfrey of the early days of television), I was an idealist, also naive. As a bedraggled child, born in Newark, New Jersey, of hardworking immigrant parents, I had been parked in the back row at school with the minority girls and boys. At Avon Avenue School, which serviced the various ghettos of the city, we were the children most ignored by the teachers.

My Italian immigrant father had worked his way through Union College, and having earned Phi Beta Kappa and Sigma Psi honors in Liberal Arts and Sciences, attended graduate school at Columbia University in New York City — among the first poor Italian immigrants to do so. Having come in steerage to America, with only the clothes on his back, he had shined shoes, delivered newspapers, carried coal buckets, tended parking lots, stacked books in the college library, slept little, gaining top academic honors with what we came to understand was near-photographic memory. He'd read the complete works of Shakespeare while working nights tending parking lots — to enhance his vocabulary — and to a mellow baritone, added American pronunciation that rivaled the famed TV news broadcaster Walter Cronkite.

Five-feet-seven-inches tall, with a pronounced limp from when he'd fallen off a table at two and dislocated his hip in the one-goat village of Candela from which he'd emigrated — he swore to vanquish anyone who might soil his daughters' honor. He'd crossed the ocean, a boy of nine alone with his mother, Lucia, her sole male protector, to be met here by his father, Galileo, already working as a shoemaker to earn passage for his family from Puglia, Italy.

My father Donato, given the name Daniel by Ellis Island officials, became the manager of a laboratory that made shortwave radio tubes for the military during World War II. He gave William Brennan, later to become a Southern media mogul, a job that had kept Brennan out of the draft and likely saved his life. In gratitude Brennan gave me an internship in his home state of Alabama at Selma's WSLA-TV, in 1961 — three years prior to the Martin Luther King Selma March and just after the first Freedom Ride.

I appeared on an otherwise all-Black gospel show, rode the back of Selma buses with Blacks that were forced to sit there, sat at the wrong end of lunch counters in the back of luncheonettes where Blacks were forced to sit, and drank at fountains marked "colored" — in a town where everything, television included, was thoroughly segregated. All hell broke loose. Crosses burned on the lawn of WSLA-TV's studio. I was arrested at midnight in my boarding house. Whereas Blacks were beaten openly in broad daylight, I was taken to a jail cell and sexually abused, by an Assistant Deputy Sheriff, a member of the Ku Klux Klan. In those days the Klan often served many a Deep South town as the law in disguise. Still sexually innocent at twenty, and unaware of the terrible danger I was in, I became an unreported casualty of the Civil Rights Movement. My association with William Brennan, the TV and radio mogul of the Deep South, might have been what kept me from being murdered as other civil rights activists were at the time.

I returned North, depressed, in a state of post traumatic stress, to finish my Bachelor of Arts degree at Montclair State College. Like Dr. Ford who brought testimony against a young drunken Brett Kavanaugh, I can remember neither the location of the jail nor of my boarding house in Selma, nor the exact time and date of sexual assault; and I never knew my assailant's name. Mostly I remember his face grinning in the dark, his slapping me for politely talking back, and the pain of penetration; his shadow in the darkness above me, and especially his reprimand: "Go back home, Yankee guinea girl, and don't come down here tellin' us Confederates who to live, eat, ride buses with, or be with on television. We like our segregated ways! Go back up there where that I-tal-i-an Sinatra dances around with that chimp jigaboo Sammy Davis Jr. Go home and live with those jigaboos you love to hang around with! Git outta Selma before we teach you a worse lesson. I can invite all of my pals to have a piece of you next time, if you don't hightail it home!"

I did leave for home and never went back to Selma. I gave up my dream of being a television broadcaster. I never told anyone of my ordeal. I was ashamed, embarrassed — as rape victims, especially women of my generation, usually are.

What could I have done to exact justice — knowing the KKK was the law in Selma and I had no good witnesses? Afraid my father, who was ill with heart disease, would have a heart attack, fearing my mother's scolding for having gone — she had not wanted me to — I said nothing. I would have destroyed my father's friendship with Bill Brennan for not protecting me. Patriarchally Italian, he was strict about my dating, never letting me stay out late, and always insisting on meeting the boys I went out with, making them pledge to protect me and bring me home safely — and early. My father cautioned me, in those days before legal abortion, to stay chaste. No good man, he said, would want a woman who wasn't a virgin. I kept my secret until the age of fifty. I published a fictionalized account entitled "The Bleeding Mimosa" in a 1995 collection of short stories. I write it here, now, as fact for the first time. The experience turned me into a lifelong activist for civil rights, women's rights, and environmental justice. My life as an activist has been documented by the prizewinning filmmaker Anton Evangelista in *Author and Activist: The Daniela Gioseffi Story*. Screened on campuses and in theaters since 2014, the film has been lauded as inspirational regarding the rights of immigrants, civil rights, women's rights, and climate justice.

Hence the motivation for this book. In these pages you will find poems, fiction, and essays by women who have suffered sexual assault, sexual harassment at work, put-downs, and general condescension for being female. Each piece is arranged in alphabetical order according to the last name of the writer. The writing is moving, empowering, enlightening, and revelatory; adding to the ever-growing #MeToo movement and the events of late that inspire more and more women to tell the truth of their lives. Statistics say that one out of three women suffers sexual assault or abuse or rape in her lifetime, and indeed most of my women friends have confessed to some form of sexual harassment or abuse. We are finally speaking out and being heard to some important degree, working toward change in the culture, more egalitarian values for all sexual identities. I'm reminded of what the accomplished Jewish American poet Muriel Rukeyser has written: "What would happen if one woman told the truth about her life? The world would split open."

And I ponder this, from the great African American Zora Neale Hurston: "There is no agony like bearing an untold story inside of you."

Then I think of the flood of breaking news stories regarding the #MeToo movement and the conversation its revelations have blasted open, creating a public forum allowing so many of us to work through past traumas, able at last to express our anger and sorrow. We realize that the culture, the sexual culture, and mores must change. We know, too, that the majority of men in our lives have acted decently, behaved honorably and ethically, that the despicable are a minority. It is not only the attacker I must forgive, to free myself of bitterness, but my own self, for having been naive in my youthful idealism.

Maya Angelou, a great African American voice of wisdom, has written: "Rape on the body of a young person, more often than not, introduces cynicism and there's nothing quite so tragic as a young cynic, because it means the person has gone from knowing nothing to believing nothing." I am happy to have averted cynicism by becoming an activist, and justifiably proud — in *Feminists Who Changed America 1963 to 1975*, published by the University of Illinois Press — that my biographical note appears alongside that of the great Supreme Court Justice Ruth Bader Ginsburg, the woman who has been so instrumental in shaping laws benefiting women. May we maintain the strength and marshal the power to defend those laws that recurrently come under threat.

The #MeToo movement helped to unleash our power. The 2016 Women's March was the largest in history. We have come to the end of shame, self-blame, and silence. We will continue to tell the truths that set us free!

Daniela Gioseffi, 2020

#ME TOO, ANCH'IO

B. Amore | Bad Dreams

The dreams were what really scared her. They were bad, very bad. When she slept at Zia Filumena's, they were the worst. She slept in a tiny narrow backroom at the top of the stairs that led to the summer kitchen and the adjacent room where her aunt and uncle slept. It was always dark in the room and she felt very alone. The rest of the rooms were empty; the flowered furniture shrouded with white covers.

Silently, those rooms pressed against her small makeshift bedroom, where she slept on the daybed. The room was high on the second floor. Sometimes if there was moonlight, she could see the branches of the big cherry tree against the sky. She knew her swing hung from the tree and that thought comforted her. Swinging in the afternoons was one of her favorite things to do, and when she began to be frightened, she would imagine swinging on the swing, so high that she nearly flew away.

But sometimes, she couldn't get away from the dream where the big shadow body moved into her bed, pressing against her back, sandwiching her body close to the wall. Then the tingling started, down the bottom of her back, between her buttocks even though her legs were tightly tucked up against her belly. She wanted to cry, but she couldn't; wanted to scream, but she couldn't. She felt like a prisoner in the dream. The black shadow took over her body and made her feel feelings she had no name for, feelings that were so strong that she was sweating when she finally woke up trembling, terrified, confused. She only knew the dream when she was in it. As soon as she woke, it was lost and she was left holding herself tight so that she wouldn't cry out. She felt paralyzed, the dream fading, leaving only the sense of her head spinning, her body stiff, and a sick feeling in her stomach.

3

She would be exhausted at daybreak, as if she hadn't slept, and she would keep her head under the covers to hide herself from the light that came too soon. She wanted more sleep, peaceful this time, with no shadow visitor and no pressure, but she felt trapped. As long as she slept in that bed, she was trapped. It was as if the shadow man knew exactly where to find her. In the mornings she felt sad, tired, and alone, and she would sometimes doze off, feeling a bit safer in the light, imagining flying up through the cherry tree where she could swing her legs free.

B. Amore | Not Spring

it was not spring
when we first made love

it was steamy summer —
the coarse wool blanket
spread on the damp forest floor

afterward, you said it was so easy
that you didn't believe
it was my first time,
and joked about deflowering

I wanted to cry —
after waiting all those years
the springtime of my virgin body —
wasted

later, as I folded up the family blanket
I figured there was not much
to do about it

had a sense that we were
moving fast towards winter,
skipping the melancholy of autumn
as fast as we'd lost the hope of spring

Amy Barone | I Quit

I quit my job of five years
so that I could watch the sun stream through the heavenly
    blue shades,
luxuriate in fresh-brewed cups of espresso from my
    kitchen,
not because my boss self-medicated with prodigious
    amounts of alcohol
and designated me his right-hand man.

I quit work that I loved and made me proud
because I needed to get reacquainted with Father Time.
I didn't leave because one day two superiors ambushed
    me,
and for hours, disparaged my work, my character, my
    essence.

I left behind a regular salary and health benefits
so that I could pop into art galleries that dot my
    neighborhood,
visit a museum for the first time in years, and catch a
    matinee.
I didn't leave because I was computer-weary from
    trafficking 400 e-mails a day.

I walked away from a family of colleagues,
people who had become an integral part of my life,
because I wanted to be a good friend again,
not because a board member cornered me one day,
grinning boyishly as he touched me where he shouldn't.

I stopped working in a chic Manhattan office building
so that I could sleep as long as I wanted every day,
walk anywhere without feeling overwhelmed,

not because I refused to sign the sham Human Resources
    papers
that put me in a bad light.

I quit my job
so that I could define myself in many ways, not one.
And after years of thinking that happiness was no more
than a fleeting moment in time,

I can heartily declare:
Happiness lives.
Happiness is freedom.

Amy Barone | Nineteenth and Sansom

My first love affair continued years later at the old
    Warwick Hotel.
Now condemned, it sits across from the Emergency Aid
    Building,
which once housed virginal girls new to Philly; a cove still
    shelters
Holy Mary, who protects gals roaming city streets.

On the block lies Sophy Curson, the boutique where my
    mother
bought pieces for her trousseau, classy clothes for the
    coveted
Niagara Falls honeymoon. Like mother's, my body
    remained intact,
but few knew we concealed continually violated souls.

Echoes of Marvin Gaye lyrics in my head, Sinatra in hers
— emboldened by pain.

Amy Barone | Summer Haze

Birthday parties in the breezeway.
Cousins galore gather 'round a bakery cake —
a huge swimming pool with sugary blue diving board.
She made every occasion special.

Yet again, he returns home from work bellowing.
We never learned how to placate the air.
My mother blamed his crazy clan.
Hours later, he's happily whistling about.

At thirteen, I get my first kiss in the backyard playhouse.
A threesome with the Stauffer twins;
my face assaulted by twirling tongues.
None of it ever like it played out in the old movies.

Grace Cavalieri | Stalked

1. How It Started

The muscular man invited her
for dinner.

Unused to romance, she
invited her husband along.

Oh, these were the days,
so innocent.

She filled her living room
with water to take a swim.

After the frolic her new friend
held her underwater.

This is not right. She spoke, but
the words floated and no one heard.

2. The Stalker

She saw Don Juan again, taking out
the garbage

her face still swollen from
pulling off the bandage.

This is why he sent her lip balm
and breath mints, orange and white.

The water of discontent
kept her away from her thirst.

If this is the only self you have
would you really give it to him?

She felt whenever someone hugged her
they didn't really mean it

but he said he did, and I think she came
to feel that nothing could destroy her.

The party was for young people
but there was that stranger again.

He ran his finger lightly under each half
of her breasts as if she wouldn't notice.

When he pretended she wasn't there
she tried to act young, although she was not.

3. Wanting Less

When needs go wrong
she needed less
until she didn't need anything at all.

The crabs in the nets
let go
trusting the dark
the way they do

dropping in like they do
when they let go.

She thought she could

master it by inviting him to lunch

get rid of him that way.

After 50 more phone calls
he talked her into dinner.

4. Ancient Rites and Modern Desires

When she was young
she always wanted
someone there waiting for her

but not this.

I make no concessions, he said, and
she wanted him to open a concession stand
to grant her some.

She looks for help — for race
creed or national origin.

The street is bare and
no one is there
but a hidden corner that's not safe.

He jumps out from a bush
grabbing her arm
saying

*When you find something
are you allowed to keep it?*

5. This Is How She Imagined Getting Away

Although
the bank

was covered
with snow
she owned
no coat
she scrambled
up without
slipping
she was not cold.

6. The Escape

Leaving the bungalow
with its melancholy rooms
she was running from
everything she saw
even the geese on the porch
the fat lady watering her lawn.

She ran toward the gray sign
with white paint
saying

7. This Way

— past the nursing home.
The twittering old ladies sit
dressing up their years of marriage
with dreams of someone coming home.

There they are in clean dresses
hair combed, talcum on the neck

talking like grown people while
becoming little girls again.

Looking for help down Route 17
not much had changed
not even the broken duck
with a wound in its side
still loping up rocks
trying to keep up.

Try as she did
she couldn't get the strong ones
away from him
no matter how much
cracked corn she imagined.

8. Telecommunication

She wore a golden whistle
Around her neck
Like a cross
Which caught
The light
Whenever she walked.

9. The End

Before the sun came up
Nature was already
Greeting a new day
With thanks for
Tender mercies.

He left like a
Squirrel twisting
His body
To make a hole

And she let it all go
Keeping only in hand what
A person can do.

10. Going Back to Work

In a dress with pink around
the hem

a dress she put on backwards

wearing shoes
with no tops

without a sweater

spilling mud splashed on papers
leaving the house in the dark

not even a light in her office
dirty walls in the room

she was so weak

her dead mother
had to come back
to make the children their lunch.

Olivia Kate Cerrone | Breaking Tradition to Save My Life

"I want to punch you in the face," my mother said. She charged at me with a raised fist. It wasn't the first time she'd tried to hit me, but I was older now and able to escape her reach.

"I'm your daughter," I said.

We stood in the living room of my childhood home. She refused to accept the news of my engagement, the reason for my visit, or the faith that my fiancé and I shared.

"He's a good man. We love each other," I said.

"Jews are selfish people. Better to be with your own kind," she said.

When I reminded her of the Sicilian American Harvard Law School graduate who hit me, she shook her head, unwilling to listen.

"What did you do to make him do that?" she said, but put up a hand, silencing me before I could respond. "We don't want to hear it."

We meant the family, the one thing they could withhold if I refused to be the good Italian American Catholic daughter they demanded, instead of one who followed her own path. My father sat on the couch, disengaged.

In my family, trauma lived in the underbrush of every interaction, prompting endless arguments and years of estrangement between relatives. Stories of abuse emerged in whispered conversations during holiday gatherings. It was accepted, for instance, that my grandfather cheated on my grandmother whenever he pleased. Often, he beat her into silence. Her own father, a fisherman from Sicily, sexually abused her. Like my nonna, my mother married young to an older, emotionally distant man in order

16

to escape a chaotic home life. My aunts and female cousins struggled with obesity, drug and alcohol addiction, leading to several tragic deaths. It was as if the women in my family were brainwashed into a patriarchal culture, having so deeply absorbed an unworthiness hammered into them, that each self-destructed.

Somewhere along the line, I also internalized this unworthiness, and spent the majority of my twenties bouncing from one abusive relationship to another, desperate to prove that I was lovable. Emotionally, I couldn't stand on my own two feet. This instability bled into other areas of my life — ruining countless friendships, jobs, and professional opportunities. Finally, in my early thirties, I found a good therapist and freed myself from the spell of self-destruction.

Abuse is cyclical, broken apart only by the cold hard clarity of awareness.

I faced my mother, whose hands no longer balled into fists. I saw her as she was, blind to the patriarchal system that imprisoned her.

"I'm leaving," I said.

"Don't call a car service at this hour of night. Haven't you heard the news? Those drivers assault women," my mother said.

Her eyes steadied on me with sincere concern. She often disassociated like this, in a frank, easy way that enabled her own survival. I turned to the window, confirming the Lyft pickup with my phone, then waited for the stranger's car to ferry me home.

Paola Corso | Girl Talk

The Triangle Factory girls say

to the Chinese girls, the Indonesian girls,
the Vietnamese, the Taiwanese

       girls girls,

take your 16-hour workday
and glue it to the sole of the shoe,

take your 20-cent-an-hour wage
and glue it to the heel of the shoe,

take the $180 he charges for the shoe
and glue it to the padding of the shoe.

And the Triangle girls say

to the Chinese girls, the Indonesian girls,
the Vietnamese, the Taiwanese

       girls girls,

take the room with 6 bunk beds
and no place to stand
and glue it to the arch of the shoe,

take the glue glue toxic glue,
burning eyes, ringing ears, bleeding nose
and glue it to the tongue of the shoe,

take the fans and vents you don't have,
gloves, masks, and aprons you don't wear

and glue them to the threads of the shoe.

And the Triangle girls say

to the Chinese girls, the Indonesian girls,
the Vietnamese, the Taiwanese

       girls girls,

take the chopsticks you can't hold
at lunch because your fingers are too numb
and glue them to the Velcro of the shoe,

take the vertigo, headaches, vomiting,
memory loss, shortness of breath, the cancer
and glue it to the glue of the shoe,

take the glue glue toxic glue
and put it under his nose, a Nike nose,
an anything-goes nose, and make him sniff.

On March 25, 1911, the Triangle Shirtwaist Company factory in New York City burned, killing 145 workers. It is remembered as one of the most infamous incidents in American industrial history, as the deaths were largely preventable — most of the victims died as a result of neglected safety features and locked doors within the factory building.

Paola Corso | In Our Hands

My father was dying of cancer.
My mother said the rosary each night before bed.
She fell asleep holding the beads. Wooden beads between
    her fingers.

I thought about how the men in my family worked their
    hands to make steel.
How the women worked their hands on the assembly line.
How they worked them in the kitchen.

My great grandmother baked bread four times a week.
She kneaded the dough, put it in a bowl, covered it with
    an old coat to quicken the rise.
When she finished, she said the rosary, a dusting of flour
    on the beads.

My mother worked in the family fruit store.
She took tiny kumquats out of their boxes,
Fingering the fruits as she laid them out in a display bin.

My sister and all her assembly line jobs.
Her hands gnarled with pain.
She can't say the rosary. She struggles to button her shirt.

The rosary is a history of working-class people.
Who couldn't afford bibles or read them.
Who wanted their prayers to count and be counted.

They got up early before work and collected pebbles.
One for every psalm from the Old Testament.
They put them in a pouch.

Pulled one out and said a prayer.
Then tossed it on the ground.
They prayed until their pouch was empty.

Instead of pebbles, a rope with knots.
Wood and clay beads.
Precious metals and gemstones.

A legend of Mary taking rosebuds from a monk's lips as he
    recited the Aves.
She wove them into a garland.
A necklace of roses. Of prayer.

Months after my father's death, I found rosary beads in a
    drawer.
I fingered them and prayed.
A garden of flowers in my hands.

Paola Corso | The Price of Eight-Dollar Jeans

Change, brother, can you spare some?

Sister is fourteen hours a day
six and seven days a week
68 dollars a month. Sister,
demanding higher
tear-gassed & slapped
back to her sewing machine,
comes home to a tin room
sees her baby one hour before bed
so little her child calls her auntie.
Sister wants to be a mother.

Say, don't you remember?

You built a factory
up to the sun that'd
last a hundred years.
Workers refuse to go in
afraid it would fall.
Go in or no pay for a month.
An hour after starting time
breaking glass cuts the air
women jump to their deaths
like our Tazreen sisters

and Triangle Factory girls
so many years ago, broken
on the ground, not in memory.

Why, brother, don't you remember?

The earth quakes, eight floors collapse
in seconds a heap of slab and iron.
Sister attaches a zipper to a pair
of denim jeans when pillars shake
around her, the floor below
heaves, she falls into cascades
of machinery and concrete.
Deep inside rubble a man's head
crushed between a beam and her thigh,
his stomach spilling out of his shirt.
Sister runs to the stairs
and falls on top of others.
Two die instantly. She passes out
wakes to cries for water.
Please, whatever you have!
A co-worker gives her urine to drink.

Brother, can you?

In the dins of sirens, fathers
from the village run the mile
through a maze of dusty lanes
past blacksmiths and the smog
of brick kilns to find their daughters.
Survivors slide down bolts
of fabric to the ground where they're
moved relay style into wheelchairs
and gurneys to hospital wards.
Rokshana, bed 47, mangled foot amputated.
Morlom, bed 48, below right elbow amputated,
Rebeka, bed 51, above left knee amputated.

Rescuers hammer through walls
and shimmy down shafts with hacksaws
to free trapped survivors who suck
the sweat on their clothes to stay alive.
Rescue me. I have two children.

I want to see them again!
Sister tries to squeeze through
a shaft but her clothes catch
on the concrete. The rescuer asks
her to take them off and extends
his hands to reach her.
Please don't hurt my breasts.
I have an 18-month-old to feed.
The man blacks out from smoke.
Sister suffocates to death.

Say you've got change, brother.

Body parts pulled out of wreckage
workers identified through
their clothing, their teeth
nose pins and keys
cell phones and prayer amulets.
Family members search for loved ones.
Give me some bones. Please,
some bones, so I can bury them.

Sister wants someone to hear her
in a crescent hole, someone to take
her out from 17 days of darkness
sipping on drips of rainwater, rationing
biscuits she bought before work
because she was too rushed to make lunch.
She hits wreckage with sticks and rods
until the sound of her tapping
is heard after a bulldozer clears rubble.
She is lifted onto a stretcher
and hooked to oxygen,
the pink scarf she wore to work
more than two weeks ago
still wrapped around her neck.

Oh, you can't change.

Families of victims
and crippled survivors
pull their children
out of school to work,
owed back pay
and compensation.
Western retailers
offer sympathy.
Police fire rubber bullets
when sister protests.

Spare some, brother.

Children's Place, Sears, Target
spare the change. Gap, J.C. Penney,
Benetton, H&M, spare the change.
Walmart, change. Change. Change
the garment industry in Bangladesh.

Hand it over, brother Rana.

Sister is done begging.

The Rana Plaza garment factory collapsed in Bangladesh on
April 24, 2013, killing 1,134 people and injuring 2,515 in the worst
disaster in the history of the global garment industry.

Donna DiCello and Lorraine Mangione | Legacy from Our Fathers

Donna & Lorraine: Inspired by the relationships with our own fathers, we spent a year interviewing Italian American women about the father-daughter relationship; their heartfelt, sad, but celebratory stories gave birth to both our research and to our book. With the #MeToo movement, these stories nudged our consciousness, and we wondered how the father-daughter relationship might be a source of strength and resilience. We offer our brief vignettes.

Donna: Empowerment comes in many forms; mine came very early in life, via my Italian American father. Though I did not realize it until adulthood, his two encouragements — to swim and to read — taught me lifelong braided lessons about the power of mind and body. He taught me to swim when I was five years old, despite my mother's protestations, at a hardscrabble beach not far from home. My father coached me to slice the water with each stroke, in tandem with wildly kicking my feet; this magically gave me the ability to propel myself forward, edging further away from him — both literally and metaphorically. In those moments I learned the power of independence and how control of one's body, and the feel of its strength contributed to that. Chronologically, I began to read around the same time, my father providing a steady supply of books for me. Once I learned how a string of words across a page made meaning and story, unimaginable worlds opened up. I read about Marie Curie, *The Island of the Blue Dolphins*, and Nancy Drew, girl sleuth. I read at night until my eyes were scratchy with sleep, wearied my mother with trips to the library, discovered poetry, and somehow knew that books and the meaning, shape, and sound of words would be both my fate and my salvation.

Lorraine: Arriving by bus on a quintessential steamy day in New Orleans, a 23-year-old in this fabled city of jazz; a layover between community organizing in Houston and a graduate school interview in Kentucky. Yes, it's a long trip, but I was determined to see New Orleans for the first time! I dashed off the bus, saw everything possible, grabbed a muffaletta for the ride, and returned breathlessly. While traversing the station parking lot, a man walked up and flashed a badge; he said he was an undercover cop, had seen me soliciting men on the streets, and I was in big trouble. Aghast, I barely understood his words as I stammered. He again described my crimes, ordering me to come with him. In the isolated sea of cars, I felt deserted. Suddenly an ancient fury hurled from me: "What are you talking about? That's crazy. Let me see that badge again." He looked at me, shocked, and disappeared instantly. I hurried inside, quickly finding an actual policeman; he and his buddy ran in pursuit. I returned to the bus. So what made me — a naïve, trusting young woman — capable of using my instinct to figure this out and escape such danger? Partly it was my internalized Italian American dad living inside me, from childhood. My dad was not a typical "tough guy" — he cried at poignant moments and his intellect was his greatest asset — but he had a strong sense of self and worth, which he gifted to me through his support, our debates, and his never-failing encouragement to stand up for what was right and true, even against rogue or fake cops.

Donna & Lorraine: Our dads — we hold their wisdom inside of us, and let that wisdom inspire us and shape us into strong women.

Jessica Femiani | Fair Warning

Before I go off to college
my mother puts her hand
on my shoulder, looks
me in the eyes. "I have to tell
you something. Women,"
she says and pauses, "Women
get raped in college. So you must be
careful. Please be very careful."

Full of care I am.
I become the protector
the watcher, the overseer
if friends have too much drink
if words begin to slur
and tears fall. And I do this
in my twenties, my thirties too
because the fear is there
of what men can do, if they
get you alone, pin you down
to the ground.

I stand in the examination room
the dermatology ward in Bologna
and the Italian doctors, the many
men, the many women, they stand
behind starched linen lab coats, electric
white, eyeglasses stern.

A voice dictates to disrobe
and I take off my shorts
the fabric crumples to the floor
and then, I pull my arms through
the neck of my shirt. I stand in my bra

my underwear; one arm cradles
the other, both arms cross my chest;
and the Italian doctors
work in pairs, gloved hands prod
and twist my arms, my legs, examine
the magenta-pink swell of my back,
the bruised welts spattered
across my back, my thighs
my arms, my chest.

And like that, the mob
of Italian doctors is gone.
And the Italian woman
doctor, with hair as thick and wavy
as my grandmother's was before
I was born, asks, *Che successo?*

It was a day at the beach
alfresco dining under the stars
at Francesca's grandmother's.
Francesca, Sabina, the grandmother,
the grandfather, my how we feasted,
laughed, our smiles wide. All the while
le tigre zanzare feasted, bites pinched
upon what my mother calls
peaches and cream. Delicate swells pink
burns red, and I dig bloody into my skin.

The Italian woman doctor's eyes
bore into me; she writes prescriptions
for steroids and creams, she tells me
Next time, you need to be more careful.
You needed to be more careful.

Jessica Femiani | An Itinerary of Action

There stands a girl of no more than five or six. She stands in the kitchen on Saturday morning. And so does there stand the girl's mother, no more than thirty-five. They stand in the kitchen together and the girl's mother will teach the girl how to make coffee. The mother shows the girl, shows the girl where the pot is kept, where the old aluminum pot is kept, with its percolator-like cap made of glass, and this pot is kept in a cabinet below the stove, on a shelf lined with other coffee-making pots. The mother shows the girl, shows her how to fill the pot with enough water. She shows the girl that enough water for two cups is right there inside, where a nut is secured to the backside of a screw, and this is where the girl should imagine the imaginary line, which tells this is as high as the water should reach. The girl must add the coffee. The ground coffee is in the tin of Chock full o'Nuts kept in the freezer. Yes, the girl takes the tin of Chock full o'Nuts from the freezer, peels the plastic lid off, and spoons ground coffee into the canister, into the aluminum canister, and yes, be sure to press light with the spoon's curve and tap, tap, tap, yes, like that, so the grains are flat. And the mother shows the girl, shows her to put the top on, screw the top of the pot back onto the pot's bottom, sit the pot on the stovetop, turn the knob, light the flame, turn the knob until the gas flame is a medium heat and then wait, wait for the water to boil, and watch for brown black to jump and poke into the glass cap. When the girl sees the brown black jump into the cap, then she is to wait a few minutes before she turns the knob to off and then tips the pot, holding the handle with a potholder; the girl streams brown black into teacups that sit on saucers, and teaspoons lay at their sides. Yes, I do not remember how the coffee in the cups traveled to the stove to the kitchen table. Was it my mother? Was it I? The certainty of memory forgotten is who it was that sat at the table's head; and my father, he may have tasted the coffee and might have said it tasted strong, weak, or maybe just right, but all that I remember is how my mother smiled proudly, for I had learned to make the coffee for my father. I learned that the doing and making for the father's pleasure is an absolute good. Yes, a girl should always make and do to please the father, the father who is also a man, a man-person to be pleased, to be made happy by the girl, and what she does and makes.

Marisa Frasca | Taking Leave

Let down my hair to cover my face
I have no black veil & must descend to the underworld
Open to pain I fear the greater pain of forgetting
That rape was not war   Don't ask me
Did I see the waste of his life   Did I accept my fate
It was not war but I could not stop dying
Now I wait for the luxury of contemplation
Let down my hair long as a curtain
I can't squander my days of passage
Let no hand extend to interrupt this grieving scene
In other words
Leave me the hell alone with the devil
For not until all hope drowns in the pool of my eyes
Trees reduce to pitiful twigs, & someone
Shuts off all the springs that feed the land, & rivers
Dry to muck & sediment, & of course
I shall never have proof
That facing the dark leads to light

Marisa Frasca | Smelling the Fox

Long ago & yesterday an orphaned fox
Entered a lonely hunter's neighborhood

Removed her skin & became woman-wife
Cooked meals, cleaned house, mothered children

Arranged flowers for the table, made money
In advertising on 7th Ave. — like you wouldn't believe

The hunter thought his wife beautiful & so crafty
He'd placed his happiness in her hands

Looked at her naked body like a body of water
For twenty years the pair merged as sea & sand

But outside of bed he always complained about her smell
Could she peel off that underlying wild musk?

Tattoo his name, rank on each of her breasts
Where's my this & my that, the food's too peppered

Got so bad, his wife schemed the perfect crime
Her midlife brain caught feral fire

She remembered foxes smell like violets
& she turned & turned depleted in her bed

Until knowing was ripe — a dream — a tree
Heavy with apples: *Eat, creature of appetite*

Her soul beneath the sheets leaped out like a bean
Jumping & howling: *Fox Fox Fox*

A hailstorm marked the road for her to follow
Deep into the forest — juggling apples on her nose

In the forest there is no deodorant. Foxes are foxes
Grace you with their presence

Marisa Frasca | Battledress

Kinswomen uncover your scars
whether slight   still oozing   or deep pit

Brocade of bruised strawberries, blood-covered rubies,
pale-pink Chantilly lace

Call on the muses to seam them together
into a battledress

Add a long train of fiery bird feathers

Hang your dress in the closet
as proof of pleasures & failures survived

Should your soul, one day, wake frozen but famished
means you've outlived a dawn
more hopeless than midnight with no moon

You've looked into your quiet mirror
& something that wants to live

begs

Open the closet   Slip on the pelt   Write!

Maria Mazziotti Gillan | In Our House Nobody Ever Said

In our house, nobody ever said you're ugly.
My sister was beautiful with her white, white skin,
her full lips, her chocolate brown eyes, her straight teeth.
She is to the right of me in this studio photo
my mother bought from a photographer who traveled
door to door in the Riverside section of Paterson.
My brother is on the left, his wide dark eyes
in his sweet face that looks solemn, self-contained,
as he does now, a doctor for more than forty years.
In the middle, I stare into the camera.
My hair a tangle of black curls, my lips formed
into a shy smile. I know that I am not beautiful.
Even then I knew it. I look like I am plugged into
an electric socket, energy crackling off
me, as though I already have things I need to do,
and I can't wait.

In our house, we all had our place:
my brother engrossed in encyclopedias my parents
    bought
on time from a door-to-door salesman,
my sister off to play baseball with the boys on 25th Street,
her body strong and athletic,
and I, who always had a book in my hand, even at the
    dinner table,
I, who found in books the life I wasn't brave enough
to live, who found in language the beauty that lifted me
out of the constraints of my world, the cold-water
    tenement apartment, the
coal stove, the raggedy linoleum, the light bulb hanging
    from a cord over
the oilcloth-covered table.

When I announced at 17 that I wanted to be a poet,
nobody ever said "You are insane. How will you earn
a living?" Instead, my mother, who sewed the lining in
        coats
in the factories of Paterson, saved pennies every week
for a year until she had enough to buy me
a pink Smith Corona portable typewriter in a pink case,
so I could be the writer she knew I wanted to be.

Maria Mazziotti Gillan | I Carry Shame with Me

How many hours have I spent drowning in shame?
Looking back, I think I lived my whole childhood
      drenched
in it — ashamed of our poverty, my immigrant parents,
my father's limp, his paralyzed leg dragging behind him,
our tenement apartment, my father's job, my own dark
      skin,
my cheap clothes, so many ways I found to hate myself,
ashamed of the life I was born to, the raggedy street,
though my mother swept the sidewalk and stoop every
      day,
though our cold-water flat was scrubbed to a shine,
nothing could change the light bulb on a cord that
      dangled
over the table, the oilcloth smell permeating the kitchen,
the girls in 7th grade who came to our house for lunch
and laughed behind their hands
at my mother's broken English.

Shame was the dress I wore
and the one I wear all these years later,
when the little girl in her hand-me-down clothes appears
and I say something as I did the other day
to a tall, slender woman. "Oh, I want your body —"
and as soon as I say it, I realize how strange I sound.
I try to explain that I meant to say
I want to be tall and slim like you, and instead
it came out like a proposition.

"That was the nicest thing anyone has said to me in years,
and now you want to take it back," she replies;
my face stained with shame, like that terrified girl

I thought I'd left behind years ago
on those cracked sidewalks of Paterson.

Daniela Gioseffi | The Erotic Furies in the News

Throughout history,
      men seem enveloped
      by sexual temptations,
      responsive to the incessant call
      of lustful desire.

Women more often look for a mate
      to make a home for family
      to feel loved in and safe.

Many men, perhaps most,
      are obsessed in a grip
      of carnal fervor
      facing arrays of ethical quandaries.

It's simple to imagine cave men
      bent on procreative urges
      with no forethought, that driving
      biological itch, but what
      of civilized men?

Why do many modern tumescent men
      do what they do?

Step into the driven male mind,
      into the reality of pure urges,
      the obstinate pressures
      of hot desires intense as sheer lunacy,

      obsession that needs to be understood
      to end wars wherein women's bodies
      are always part of power's booty —

since the dawning of homo sapiens,
since Aeschylus's Suppliant Women,
since the Rape of the Sabine Women,
abducted Comfort Women for Japan's Army,
the ongoing global trade in sexual slavery,
the Hollywood audition couches,
the constant rape of women in war,
      women's bodies as the bounty
            of male power.

Daniela Gioseffi | Eve Talks with Mother Earth Who Swallowed the Blood of Her Beloved Son Abel

You opened your mouth to him, Mother,
    and took him in.
Are you comforting Abel in your belly?
Will he fertilize the Tree of Life
    for all of us?

God gives no peace to Cain.
He sends him out of His sight in pain
to wander in a World of Death and Sorrow.

Though one still lives, I grieve
    the loss of both my sons.

Mother Earth, when will the testicular
God of War give us peace? We give birth in pain
and God takes our sons away forever.

After so much toil and nursing to raise them,
He spills their blood and cripples them
    in useless wars, and they pillage you,
    Mother, for things that do not
                make them happy.

What they really desire is the safety of our arms.
They call for us as they die on the battlefield.
Mama, Mother, Mommy, Mom, they cry out!

They want our milk in their mouths, not blood,
but they don't understand their anger
    in growing away from us into men
    who must toil for their bread.

Maria Giura | At Fifteen

At fifteen I got my first job at a restaurant,
a block away from Macy's.
I took the subway
to Manhattan,
emerging from Penn Station
in my skirts,
on summer mornings that were hot by nine,
to ring up plates of baked ziti and eggplant parmigiana
for the lunch crowd.

I was so excited —
clutching my pocketbook,
smoothing my skirt —
until I turned the corner
and saw the men
crawling from the backs of their trucks.

"Beautiful blue eyes, baby. Where'd you get *those*?"
one of them hissed,
while the others smacked
the air with vulgar kisses.
I felt like the woman
in the photograph
American Girl in Italy,
her eyes downcast,
gripping her scarf.

I kept my head up,
careful not to look
them in the eye,
smiling,
so I wouldn't seem rude.

Maria Giura | Rockin' Eve

It's New Year's
and we're at my sister's,
the ball already dropped,
the fire roaring,
Martini & Rossi still in our glasses.

Rockin' Eve is on in the background.
A split screen shows on one side
Carrie Underwood and Miley Cyrus
in crushed velour caps,
lyrics pouring from their mouths.
And on the other, Dick Clark
struggling to pull up his words
while thousands below him scream.

By now my nephews
have disappeared to the basement
with their toy guns.

Only the girls have stayed back to sing
around my niece's karaoke machine.

I draw close to them —
these girls
who share my DNA —
and sing
Life's what you make it, so let's make it rock
when I catch my sister's mother-in-law
stare at me from the couch.
I know her long enough — twenty years —
to know what she's thinking:

What a shame Maria never married.

She means well,
but her stare triggers the self-pity
I thought I had under control,
so I sing louder,
trying to drown it out,
wishing it could be as easy as nine years old again —
not that everything at nine is easy.
Still, you can dance in a circle of girls
at a New Year's party,
throw your lungs into a pop song,
and really believe the lyrics.

Maria Giura | Mary

I like the Blessed Mother
when she's not being assumed,
coronated, glorified,
put on a shelf
like a china doll.

I like my Mother Mary earthly,
with the Babe in her arms,
sandals firmly planted
in Nazareth,

and her face,
instead of demurely bowed, blazing,
declaring to Elizabeth:
From this day all generations will call me blessed.

I like my Mother Mary with long hair
and a headband,
her eyes fixed on the Baby,
on us, like the statue
in the church near my sister's in Rochester,
that looks more flesh than plaster
and has no title or at least none
we can figure out.

I need my Blessed Mother human,
for when I look at her
I think there might be a chance for me
pregnant with
every kind of fear,
every kind of dreaming.

Roxanne Marie Hoffman | Girls' Night Out

Lyrics sung at *Rockin' the Mic Against Rape* with Susan Yung simultaneously reading news articles and rape statistics, Bowery Poetry Club, New York City, 2006. Commissioned by the New York City Alliance Against Sexual Assault.

It's time to be beautiful!
It's time to get girly!
We're gonna go strut our stuff!
So Daddy, please don't wait up —
We won't be home early!

Let's kick off our combat boots!
We'll let down our hair!
Step into the stilettos,
You know that black patent leather pair.

There's time for a manicure,
A pedicure too;
Maybe retouch that gray,
And try out a new do.

Let's whip out the lip gloss
And glitz up with glitter;
Don't worry about Dad and the boys;
We'll just call the sitter.

Let's shed the sweatshirt
And unveil the halter;
I bet Dad will propose again —
If his heart doesn't falter.

Let's squeeze on the miniskirt
And show some leg;

We'll practice our flirting
And make the boys beg!

It's time to be beautiful!
It's time to get girly!
We're gonna go strut our stuff!
So Peter, honey, please don't wait up —
We won't be home early!

We're going to have a girls' night out!
And leave the men home;
Tonight, there will be no doubt
That we are real women!

Tonight, we will flout
All man-made-up rules;
And any guy who messes
With us is just an unschooled fool!

We like to choose our men,
And be wined and dined,
And then say *if* and *when*;
We make up our own minds!

Don't try to push us around
'Cause we'll push back;
Please ask us nicely,
And show us some tact.

If you treat us like Goddesses,
We might treat you like Gods;
But if you make yourself a pest,
We won't give you a nod.

We try to be diplomats
And not hurt your pride;

So when we say "No way, Jose!"
Please take it in stride.

When we say no we don't mean maybe,
When we say no we aren't playing hard to get.

You may say: "So sorry, baby . . .
Just one of those things
That doesn't mean anything;
Just some fun with no regrets."
We may forgive you, but we never forget!

Don't make us wield baseball bats
And squirt pepper spray.
And trying to get us drunk?
Well, it's not okay.

Let us be the gentler sex,
And love us tender,
Or we'll send you off to jail,
Proclaimed sex offender!

Maria Lisella | #MeToo May Be Changing Lives, but Can It Change Behavior in the Workplace?

Recently, #MeToo stories have appeared on social media platforms following an all-too-familiar script: a prominent man is accused of impropriety. He faces public shaming via Twitter and maybe disavowal from the company he keeps or runs. The fury and outrage go viral. And then?

If accusers take legal action, the burden of proof is on them: she or he would have to carefully construct a case based on facts that illustrate a pattern of behavior; and while eyewitnesses are rare, at least the testimony of those who saw the victim shortly after the incident may be called upon to attest to his or her claims.

The phrase "sexual harassment" was coined in 1975 by Working Women United, a group led by journalist Lynn Farley that included Carmita Wood, a 44-year-old mother of four who was denied unemployment benefits after quitting her administrative assistant position in order to escape the unwanted advances of her immediate supervisor, the director of Cornell University's nuclear laboratory. Wood had contacted Farley for assistance in her appeal, and Working Women United was organized in an effort to bring attention to Wood's plight and other similar injustices.

Five years later, in 1980, the Equal Employment Opportunity Commission (EEOC) would determine that sexual harassment is sex discrimination (and therefore prohibited by Title VII of the Civil Rights Act of 1964), defining sexual harassment as "unwelcome offensive sexual behavior, either physical or verbal, which embarrasses, humiliates or intimidates co-workers or subordinates."

Another six years, in 1986, the Supreme Court would uphold the findings of the EEOC, ruling that speech in itself could create a hostile environment and violate the law, in the landmark case of *Meritor Savings Bank v. Vinson.*

In the '90s, Congress would pass the Civil Rights Act of 1991, the Violence Against Women Act of 1994, and the Government Accountability Act of 1995, each providing an additional layer of protection for working women.

To comply, governments — from federal to local — as well as corporations, universities, and the military developed policies and pamphlets that defined sexual harassment and distributed them among employees and employers. The Civil Rights Act was enacted in 1964, but it would not be until the mid-1970s that the first sexual harassment cases were brought to court under the act, and not until the mid-1980s that sexual harassment was recognized by the Supreme Court as sex discrimination; and not until the '90s that plaintiffs were given the rights to a jury trial in Federal court and to collect compensatory and punitive damages, that the use of plaintiff's past sexual history as evidence was limited, and that Congress's own members became subject to the same employment laws as the rest of the country.

Back then, when social media did not exist, public forums were limited. Legal recourse led to settlements often involving the loss of a job (for the victim not the offender). A settlement compensating the claimant would also buy their silence regarding the names of offenders or the establishments they worked for.

A few years after sexual harassment was formally recognized, I was fired from a job I loved as a labor journalist and found myself testing the new laws.

With #MeToo as a backdrop, I hope my own experience inspires more solutions about the methods we employ to fight sexual harassment and to achieve change in the workplace.

Where we are now: Society is talking and listening. Sexual harassment claims won't be dismissed as quickly as in the past. Yet, victims still carry the burden of proof. Developing carefully constructed cases may be arduous, but may empower accusers rather than shame them.

Because not all cases are alike and not all claims are against high-profile offenders, I followed the rules of legal discourse; worked with a lawyer; won a settlement, albeit behind closed doors, in a private session.

Looking back, the victory seemed hollow and lacked satisfaction or even complete closure for a cluster of reasons, not the least of which, I was without a job, the offender kept his high-paying position, and I was paid off to cover damages and ensure my silence.

***

I would like to share how I constructed my own case back in the 1980s, when the lines were clearly drawn within legal boundaries and the forums were for the most part, private. Mine was an ordinary case, not set in a glamorous industry, nor would it garner any public attention.

I was working as a labor union journalist in St. Louis, Missouri, on an assignment that included an overnight stay at a hotel.

After the day's meetings, I joined other rank and file members and executives at a bar. There, a VP from the union made explicit sexual remarks. I had often been in the company of men, as the union members were predominantly male, but the rank and file treated me with respect. It was the executives who took liberties.

I documented every remark the VP made in case I would have to defend myself. That night my phone rang incessantly, someone kept knocking on my door. In short, I not only had already been harassed but also now was being intimidated.

Not long before, I had taken a course on sexual harassment through the Working Women's Institute.

Now I was in a position to test the parameters. At twenty-six I was scared, but I wanted to fight back.

When I returned to the union headquarters, my home base, I was summoned to the president's office. He had already tried to kiss me once behind closed doors, but I ducked. He told me to close the door, although one of the rules of combat is: never be alone with a potential offender.

"If you must be in the room alone with your offender, be sure someone outside that door can testify you were upset upon leaving," another rule I bore in mind.

The president's secretary saw me going in and storming out of his office. I was officially fired because in the president's words, "I got reports from the VP that you are speaking out against the union."

This came out of left field, but the VP decided to strike before being struck. When I told the president about the bar incident, he replied with, "You expect me to believe that?" At that point, I shouted across his desk, "You fired the wrong woman!"

Simultaneously, my assistant was trying to organize the mostly female clerical workers, an action the president had wrongfully attributed to me. Her action followed the announcement that the union would pick up stakes and move the headquarters to the right-to-work state of Tennessee. Most of the office workers were women who were within three months of being vested for their pensions.

The offender was so arrogant that many of the incidents of harassment took place publicly — in the office cafeteria, the hallways, and in meeting rooms. When I asked other women to testify, class divisions emerged.

The professional women at the union refused to testify though they had witnessed incidents and were often victims, much like the audience at the recent Academy Awards Night in Hollywood.

The women who came forward in my defense were the secretaries, the clerks. These women had endured his behavior and were happy for a chance to be heard and vindicated. They also had no reason to compromise any longer with a management that was about to deny their pensions.

My case was filed with the Human Rights Commission and the National Labor Relations Board. I prepared detailed statements for both agencies; I collected testimonies to illustrate patterns of behavior.

The offender was so incorrigible that while we waited outside the door of the Human Rights Commission, he winked at my lawyer and said, "Hiya, sweetheart," as she leaned over and whispered, "I cannot wait to get this guy in front of an administrative judge."

My award for compensating damages was modest. Although I signed a statement that indicated I would never name names, I appeared on a TV news program shortly afterward.

With face blacked out and name withheld, I told viewers that sexual harassment was an occupational hazard; that it happens to women of all ages, races, and professions — mothers, sisters, daughters, and girlfriends; that it takes the form of looks, innuendos, touching; and creates a hostile atmosphere that threatens women's livelihood. And I hoped I was heard.

***

An endless parade of public figures — from Hollywood mogul Harvey Weinstein, to FOX News commentator Bill O'Reilly, to soft-spoken liberal Charlie Rose, and more recently Pulitzer Prize-winning novelist Junot Diaz, and star chef Mario Battali — have been called out for bully behavior and far worse. To date, over 250 celebrities and other high-profile individuals have been accused of sexual misconduct ranging from harassment to assault. Twenty-five women have accused Donald Trump, current President of the United States, of sexual misconduct.

The methods used to call attention to such incidents, however, did not start or end behind closed doors with administrative judges and lawyers presiding over the cases but on Twitter, Facebook, websites, and blogs.

How sexual harassment has been spotlighted has deeply divided even the staunchest supporters of the victims.

My question is: Do these abbreviated messages educate or inform the public or do they just heighten tension and more misunderstandings? Are these effective methods to bring about the change we seek? Are the tweets dividing public opinion? Are the posts watering down the seriousness of the charges?

Assuming the long-range goal is to pressure potential offenders from behaving badly, are shame-producing social media posts capable of effecting that change or is the more traditional route, i.e., filing legal documents the way to go?

Admittedly, posts have instigated public conversations and captured media attention, but are they enough to raise public consciousness?

Further, sexual harassment is complex: do all victims feel the same rage, damage; and are all offenders alike?

If a person steals a pack of gum from a candy store or steals a car, the person is still stealing. Likewise, if a person uses their position to press another into a trap of unwelcomed sexual attention, whether that manifests itself in a kiss or rape, the offender is still employing the same tools — power, prestige, dominance — to have his or her way.

While Junot Diaz was cleared by MIT and allowed to return to the university to teach, Harvey Weinstein was sentenced to twenty-three years in prison for rape and sexual abuse. As we continue to hear news of allegations and convictions, we are forced to consider the cumulative impact on women's livelihoods and our society, by both the crimes and the coverage, official or unofficial.

The current cases may have muddied the playing field for accusers and facile social media activists. As a first line of attack, could social media posts undermine the construction of legitimate legal cases, which can be arduous but perhaps a more effective method of defense?

We know sexual harassment is about domination and power. What we have not defined yet is what forums we need to employ to continue bringing pressure on models of bad behavior and how to go forward.

Not all women will have the advantage of having high-profile jobs that garner media attention, so how best to make sure sexual harassment does not go unnoticed? How best to bring about the consciousness, the mindfulness necessary to bring about change in the workplace?

As one chef who found herself in the maelstrom of enduring harassment as a price for success, Traci Des Jardins, a former contestant for "Top Chef Masters" in 2011, told *The New York Times*: "We're not past it by any means, but it's time to focus on the people who are doing it right. And there are plenty of them."

Resource: Nancy P. Condit, "Working Women's Institute Publicizes Battle Against Sex Harassment," *The Oklahoman*, April 8, 1985.

Joanne Monte | A Delicate Balance

I'm imagining where you might be
at this hour — standing before the bureau,
exercising your lean muscle
with the weight of choosing to lift
either the nightshirt
or the lace, trying for balance
like the women before you
learning to dance,
bounding with air in the warm light;
or like the wives seen in the vineyards,
hauling baskets of grapes
as clear as amethysts on their thin shoulders.
I imagine that in this hour your fingers
will lightly snap the rose from the vine,
and then twist the key
in the hurricane lamp for the glow
that will keep you in its eye.
I imagine how in the morning
you will move in a natural light
to throw open the doors of your wardrobe,
rummaging through the pin-striped suits,
vests, trousers, the sea-captain's jacket
and the washed-down jeans. I can hear
your voice humbled, rising from
the back of your throat. *Why
haven't women been given to rule
the world?* And I sit at my desk,
thinking that I, too, can try for balance
even at this late hour to answer your question.

Joanne Monte | Behind the Screen

of morning glories, a young woman
    keeps to her promise
        where she has taken refuge
            passing from the darker side of blue

into an alcove, into a spiritual glimmer
        that catches the eye of the robin.

There are ice tints on the lake; a full moon
        in mother-of-pearl, slipping out

        of obscurity. Geese
           migrate in and out of the scrolls

into a world of solemn blue and gold,
    filling the gap that we had forgotten.

She moves beyond them,
    seeking a reversal of power, hoping to rise above

        the fanned-out wings of butterflies,
        beyond the sweet plum

and persimmon and into another realm —
    creating a new world from within.

Kathryn Nocerino | Losing My Religion

I tell anyone who asks what my religion is that I am a confirmed atheist. This is a matter of fact. Having been raised Roman Catholic, I experienced two sacraments: Communion and Confirmation; ergo, Confirmed Atheist. There is a professional photo of me somewhere — unless I've burnt it — as a small child, taken after my First Communion. In it I wear all white — veil, dress, gloves, little bouquet — just like some tiny underage thing getting ready to become the eighth bride of a cult leader. My expression was one of total "What, me worry?" unconsciousness, the expression Trump voters undoubtedly wore pulling the lever in the voting booth.

Actually, it was a veil, not the one in the photograph, from that white ensemble which cost my parents so much in the rampant-Catholicism supply store, but the little thing I was required to wear in the old St. Michael's in Queens, during Sunday mass. My mother and I had to put these veil-ettes on, but I noticed that none of the men and boys had anything on their heads. Pinning it on for the first time, at around the age of four or five, I felt conspicuous. "Why do I have to wear this?" I asked my mother. I don't remember what she said, probably something along the lines of "because." Because the sun rises every morning. Because water doesn't flow uphill. Because because because.

I sometimes wonder what females in other organized religious communities feel about having to don the *chador* or sit in a gallery behind a curtain apart from their male counterparts in the *shul*. Just yesterday, I heard that someone quit a group, in disgust, when its Religious Authority endorsed female genital mutilation as a cure for hypersexuality. Where I come from, hypersexuality is encouraged. To hell with Organized Religion; up with

Disorganized Religion; all available evidence proves the latter is much more fun.

I remember that for me the main roadblock in Math was my steadfast refusal to accept the Axioms. I went on strike; I decided to stick to my guns until somebody proved them to me. Well, the Catechism reminded me of the Axioms. The Catechism was something you were made to repeat until you could recite it from memory. Once memorized, it was supposed to become part of you.

When I started Sunday School classes, which dragged me out of public school every Wednesday in the middle of the day — all of my non-Catholic schoolmates staring at me as I left — I learned that women were created by God from one of Adam's ribs; and that the first woman, Eve, cursed all of us with Original Sin by allowing Satan, in the guise of a snake, to persuade her to chomp on the Apple of Knowledge and then hand it to Adam. Goodbye, Garden! Hello, working for a living! When I first heard this story I thought there was something wrong with it, but I couldn't say what.

A year later, in Biology I, they informed us that children got born, and moreover, got born due to gene sharing between the parents. In school they told us knowledge was good and you had to accumulate as much as possible; in church they said knowledge is bad and you had to avoid it at all costs. Faith! Don't think; just have Faith; God will show you the way. I understand that lots of people live like that. Just look at the voting statistics. Life, at worst, can be a fearful thing, and it invariably concludes in Death. How tempting complete certainty is. All you have to do is disavow independent thought. You don't wanna be a Freethinker, do you? Huh? Huh? Again, lots of people . . .

Then I found out I couldn't be Pope. I was your basic ambitious kid; I wanted to Be the Best that I Could Be. But there was no possibility of advancement in the

Church. I could, of course, become a nun, which meant life sentence in a convent, wearing black from head to toe, and no pension. Hey, just dump the old lady in a wheelbarrow! No *extremely* decorated apartments in the Vatican; no alb, no mitre, no robes with Threads of Gold, no adoring crowds, no Popemobile! Not only couldn't I be Pope; I couldn't even be a priest! "Keep that thing on your head!" my mother said as I tried to scratch an itch.

Despite a growing sense of injustice, I kept attending mass. I believe that I attended purely for aesthetic reasons. Before our brownstone church was condemned for structural instability, it was an immersive journey into the past. The church was dark inside, the only real light streaming in through Tiffany windows — windows in which, as floating clouds created shadows and the light flickered, the figures seemed to breathe. Then there was the odor of incense and the sound of bells. Then there was the boys' choir. Then there was the Latin Mass. Until St. Michael's was torn down. Its replacement was a bleached oak, California A-frame, brightly lit inside, mass in English, and a priest with a guitar leading the congregation in folk songs. I turned on my heel and left for good. If I wanted folk songs, I could hear really good examples in Washington Square Park, songs about murder, songs about ghosts, songs that could make your hair stand on end.

But it wasn't until age thirteen that I developed enough courage to admit that I didn't believe in God. For many years I suspected as much but would not yield. I must have Faith, I thought. I strained, and I strained, like someone who eats a diet with insufficient fiber. I am not sure what finally did it: the perceived injustice, the secular classwork, or the mere fact that I seem to run on logic. Yes, cars run on gas; I run on logic. I told my mother: "I don't believe in God." She replied: "You're only being difficult." She also said: "Wait till you get old. Everybody suddenly gets religious when they're old." My father, however — out of earshot — admitted to being an Agnostic. He also told me that my grandfather had been an atheist, and moreover, an atheist to the point of blasphemy. "Lies!" he would yell in Neapolitan. My grandfather would reportedly tell my Milanese grandmother she was an idiot for going to church. That, I thought, could not have been a happy marriage.

The nuns used to say that God would strike you down with a bolt of lightning for blasphemy. The word they would have used in biblical times was "smite." I went outside, figuring that the bolt of lightning would mess up my parents' Castro convertible. I don't remember what particular blasphemy I uttered, but I just stood there and nothing happened. Well, I thought, that's that.

Today I am a very mellow type of atheist. I am content in my godlessness, so much so that I do not see the need to proselytize. My hope is that people, left to their own devices, will eventually come to their senses. For this reason, I would never legislate religion out of existence. We all know what happens when the Government prohibits something.

Kathryn Nocerino | Wimmin in the Arts

Z. Budapest, a Hungarian author, activist, journalist, playwright, and songwriter living in America, promoted the use of *wimmin* as a feminist spelling of women (with *womon* as the singular form) in the 1970s.

Studying at Cooper Union in the '6os, fresh out of mysterious, cosmopolitan Flushing, I thought that bars were dens of vice and iniquity. I wasn't quite solid on what iniquity was, but I was dead certain it lived inside of bars. I came from a family that really didn't drink. Of course, my paternal grandfather, The Holy Terror, was an exception, but my parents' idea of risk involved ¼ of a glass of sweet vermouth consumed with meals as an appetizer.

One of my classmates said, "Let's go to this bar in Soho." Now, at that time, Soho had not yet collapsed under the weight of gentrification. Artists lived there illegally, jerry-rigging lofts with extremely non-compliant plumbing and electrical gizmos. There were only a handful of eating and drinking establishments, most of them carryovers from the last century, Italian and Irish hangouts for the working class. Now, of course, Soho is *haute bohème*. Artists are like ants: they move into an area, start doing what they are best at, i.e., making the old new again, and bingo! Before they know it, they're out on their asses. Why, even Donald Trump and some nice people from Georgia, in what used to be called the USSR, got into the game. Thank your neighborhood artist.

This particular bar was a new addition, housed in a ground floor loft on, let's say, Wooster Street. As befitting a den of vice and iniquity, the walls were painted black, floor to 20-foot ceiling. Since it was only late afternoon, the place was virtually empty. Only two people leaned against the bar rail: a twentyish man and a much older woman. Somehow I couldn't take my eyes off of her. Very tall, unsmiling, a square, dour face which looked as if it had been hacked out of granite: a Picasso sculpture, or Judith Anderson playing Medea. She wore flowing garments that looked like priestess robes, made of very expensive fabrics in charcoal and black. Her piercing black eyes regarded us once, then turned their unsettling gaze on her young companion. I noticed, faintly shocked, that the woman wore extremely long fur eyelashes.

"Do you know who that is?" my classmate asked under his breath. I didn't. "That's Louise Nevelson," he said, "a total bitch. She eats male artists like candy." I would have thought witch rather than bitch. Whatever she was, she virtually radiated power.

At that time, and only to a slightly lesser extent today, prominent women artists were as rare as eating and drinking establishments in Soho. Of course, I entered Cooper Union to become a Woman Artist. Apparently, it wasn't that simple. It seems that a woman artist was a freak of nature, a two-headed giraffe, a flying refrigerator, the Loch Ness Monster. The phrase goes, *kinder, kirche, kuche.* I have no interest in children; organized religion gives me hives, and the only thing I tend to do in the kitchen is raid the refrigerator. My head swam. What have I gotten myself into, I wondered, holding my head. But then again, this is simply what I do. Cats have kittens; I have art works. I'm sorry. I apologize profusely. I prostrate myself to the ground and, to demonstrate remorse, hit my head on the floor: *ka-BONK! ka-BONK! ka-BONK!* But there is nothing I can do about it. It occurred to me that this is how people used to get burnt at the stake, and in some locales to this day, stoned to death. Women Artists: An Abomination Before God.

"In order to make it as an artist," one of my fellow students said, "you have to be a bitch." He had looked intently at me. "I don't think you've got it."

Several of the other [male] students, once in their cups, would drone on and on about the artist/muse equation. "A woman can't be an artist," they would drawl, "because she has to be a muse."

"What's a muse?" I said.

Also, galleries and museums didn't like to exhibit work by women unless they absolutely had to. The Bible could have said, "It is easier for a camel to pass through the eye of a needle than it is for a woman to get a gallery show." Women artists, other than people like Louise Nevelson, God bless her, couldn't pull off the languid, cock-of-the-walk pose so favored among successful male artists, a cachet that apparently attracts buyers as well as groupies. Male artists are expected and encouraged to be full of themselves; women are encouraged to be wallpaper. Here is another mantra that was making the rounds at the time, invariably uttered as a "joke": "women are better obscene than heard." An all-time favorite would begin like this: use "horticulture" in a sentence. You would comply and the guy would yell, "WRONG! It goes like this: *You can lead a whore to culture but you cannot make her think!*" An ear-to-ear grin, the grin that comes when you trash 51 percent of the world's population, would always accompany this piece of crap. A woman artist is, in point of fact, as welcome as a nun brandishing a ruler.

But I am nothing if not incorrigible. I am one of those crazies in a speeding car who sees a brick wall pop up in the middle of a racecourse and says, "To hell, I'm drivin' thru it!"

In the middle of my freshman year, McSorley's Day rolled around. "Wow!" my male classmates started saying, three weeks in advance, "It's coming up!" Some people use Advent Calendars; Cooper Union students counted on their fingers till McSorley's Day. Finally, there it was. What exactly was McSorley's Day? It was a day when you entered

McSorley's and drank as many beers as your innards could accommodate. My plan was to order a ginger ale and watch as the rest of them got ridiculous. We veritably skipped toward the venerable bar, a narrow establishment sunk like a decaying molar into the façade of an equally debilitated tenement building. We walked in. Looking around me, I thought the place gave the term "dive" meaning and splendor.

Suddenly the barkeep put down his rag and pointed: "YOU! Out!" I looked around me. Was he throwing us out? Were we dressed improperly? Sneaking a glance at a 300-year-old rum-dum canted sideways on one of the back chairs, either sleeping or drunk to the point of unconsciousness, I didn't think so. One of my classmates nudged me in the ribs. "He means you. Women aren't allowed in McSorley's." Of course it was me. It was always me.

I would like to remind the reader that this is the same McSorley's immortalized by the great *New Yorker* writer, Joseph Mitchell, in his collection *Up in the Old Hotel*. Mitchell spent hours listening to and buying drink after drink at McSorley's for people like Joe Gould, Professor Seagull, and who knows how many other geezers and tosspots, then transforming their conversations into pure journalistic gold. Nobody threw Mitchell out.

Years later I found out that a woman owned McSorley's. Now the place admits women, but only because a law was enacted that made them do so.

I worked hard, very hard. The brick wall loomed up repeatedly, but I disregarded it. One professor of drawing likened my work to Lautrec's, another to that of Alfaro Siqueiros. I got a painting into one Cooper Union Annual and an etching with aquatint into another. The head of the company that made the giant mechanical signs in Times Square bought the print. One of my professors, the inventor of the first sans serif typeface, bought a kinetic sculpture. It turned out that I was the only student who had actually sold anything.

Cooper Union's lone bohemian engineering student wrote a poem to me in which he compared me to the Mona Lisa: "Mona Lisa, tripping on the staircase, death defying . . ." I disregarded it.

At the close of my time at Cooper Union, because I had no marketable skills, I applied to graduate programs for an MFA. My portfolio looked like the work of five different artists because, unlike my classmates, I had come so late to the game. Everyone else had started out at the High School of Music and Art, or a similar feeder institution, and had developed a unified style. Harvard accepted me for a degree in Art History but did not offer me financial support.

I got a marriage proposal from one of my fellow students, someone I had actually never dated. He offered me a really great deal: I could get a job in a supermarket and work while he built his career as a Famous Artist. This was a life script I heard being discussed over and over in the lunchroom. The men would do Art while the women got some kind of job. It would be *kinder, kuche, cashier.* "What about my career?" I shrieked at the top of my lungs. "Well, you can do it later," he said.

Did I marry the guy? No. Did I become a Famous Artist? No. But, I am extremely proud to relate, I did turn into a bitch.

Angelina Oberdan | How I Can't Forget

How before dinner, we had drinks, watching our dogs wrestle in the yard. How he held my dog to the ground with his knee, that's how the dog would learn to mind. He said it needed it, needed to learn. How he told me about his baby son, dropped off at his parents. They wanted to meet me if this worked. How he offered drugs and I took them: easy, a small pill on my tongue, a swallow. How later, after dinner, he said how beautiful I was without a shirt as I perched topless on the countertop, and how he took pictures so that he could show me how he saw me, beautiful. How when we kissed, his teeth tugged at my lower lip, and he led me by the hand onto the bed's white cotton sheets, and it seemed enough. Then, how he told me I was terrible, no good at all, a slut, a bad one, how I left the room to drink one more beer, to check on my dog, to sleep on the couch.

How, the next morning, I couldn't move to leave, naked, tossed under an oversized throw. How he cleaned up while I lay on my side and watched; how he wiped down the counters, bleached the sheets. How I guess I eventually pulled on my jeans. How the dog climbed into the backseat, how I could barely sit to drive, how I just kept puking. How I made it home. How I showered, and how in the mirror, I found my collarbone dotted in bruises. I think that's when I was sure. How I held up in my house, and I packed myself with ice. My dog stayed protectively curled at my feet.

Angelina Oberdan | Vulture

As I leave your driveway for the last time,
a turkey vulture picks sinew from a squirrel's bones
in the yard of the house I am abandoning. My car is weary,
full, packed heavy with clothes on hangers,

dishes in broken boxes, and what else I own.
The vultures are always around,
often perched together on the vacant seams
of houses, a committee of hunched brown shades

waiting to begrudge the dead of its last meat.
Pausing to adjust the rear view, before heaving away,
I watch a vulture pinning the corpse with its talons,
twisting the loose spine to entrée what's left.

This is what you have done to me; carved out my skull.
Your tough beak repeatedly strikes my bone.

Lisa Marie Paolucci | Birth

I begged the young man to numb my pain
and was confined to the wide white bed
as the emptiness spread across my thighs.
Leaning on my left hip, then right, as instructed, I waited.

The doctor was with someone else when my body took
    control.
I heard her screaming.
The waves rolled on their own,
and the nurse admonished me not to push yet, doctor's
    orders,
but it could not be stopped.

And when the doctor finally worked his way down the
    hall,
stood between my legs, and thought I wasn't moving fast
    enough,
my vagina was sliced open, the head began to emerge, and
    he came,
beautiful and swollen, red cheeks, sweet curious eyes.

But I could not gaze lovingly as I felt the needle pierce my
    skin,
over and over,
the doctor sewing me back together,
recreating my shape.

Noticing my wincing, he said he couldn't believe I could
    feel that.

Michelle Reale | *Ormai* (By Now)

I was never lonely until the day
you caught me in the murky blue
of your eyes, the look that settled

over me like a velvet fog. The things the mind
and the body remember: I, in my white
crisp blouse with the retro Peter Pan collar;

the polished tip of your Italian-made shoes, the precision
of your shave; the mottled flush of my neck that
you mistook for coy desire.
                          You deserve the best.
Years later, I made excuses. Maybe you
were the victim of malignant mothering; maybe
your sister, a silhouette nailed to the crumbling wall,

inconsequential, perennially unheard. And I, under
   constant scrutiny,
already a foothold in stubborn self-hate; my own one-
   sided account
with no witness, no one to speak on my behalf.
                          Baby.
What I understood, what I saw, what I knew still grows in
   me, leaps
from one inscrutable outburst to the next. Anger bleeds
   into
the four corners of the pallid room.

Watch me now in my nautilus as my chambers curl
in on one another, an indelicate overlay, the background
   of
my life ever since.

You'd think I'd have forgotten it by now. I live in between
      the riddles
and rebukes.

By now, you are onto someone else in the drab
industrial-carpeted hallways of a midsize house.
There you will groom a woman, similar to me, to make
the coffee while convincing her of the comfort it adds
to your day. After all, if you are successful, aren't we all?
              Honey.
By now, you would think I'd have forgotten the touch of
      your hand on my neck like an intimate strangulation,
      the fiddling of my gold crucifix on the delicate
      scaffolding of my chest, and the strong rebuke
which I could always count on afterward, which confused
      and panicked me. Your wife on line one and my acid
      stutter as I tell her that you are (still) in a meeting.

              Still? He should have been done by now!
You told me I was the type of woman who would
jump into fire for a man. But I wasn't. Here is what I know
      now:
For many women, just to live is to burn.

I want to voice a regret. I want to tell you, that by now, you
      should understand you never even knew me. Not at all.

Nina Carey Tassi | Esther in Her Nakednes

On Jerusalem's noisy Via Dolorosa,
hawkers in the marketplace drown out
ancient days, till I step into a quiet shop
glowing with Byzantine icons.

Treasures at every glance, I exchange
smiles with the Armenian owners;
a spell drifts over me.

Then, framed in gold, she appears —
a young nude of radiant beauty,
her gaze transparent.

She could be Botticelli's *Venus*,
but I ask, heart pounding, *Is this Esther?*
The owner smiles, *Yes.*

Queen Esther, secret Jewess in exile,
overcame king's power, saved her people
from slaughter, won Bible's praise for all ages.

Now I see her in a new light, naked,
no gossamer cloth for virginal modesty,
a shocking detail at her feet: a servant kneels,
wrapping a silk ribbon around one ankle.

In Esther's open gaze, innocence resides,
not yet taken from her, to be sorely ripped
away in the royal bedchamber.

The silk ribbon foreshadows
Esther's awakening to knowledge,

searing moment of shame she will face,
hidden by the artist from the young virgin.

The moment will not come
as she stands trembling at the king's door,
nor steps into his chamber and sees his body,
loosely draped, grossly large.

The moment will not come
as he gestures to her maid to remove
Esther's robe and leave them; not even
as she endures his ogling.

The moment will come
when the king with glittering eyes
beckons her, and she walks leadenly
over to his bed, protest futile,
forced harlotry begun.

This artist clearly fell in love
with Esther's innocent beauty,
couldn't bear to show her suffering,
sensing she never forgot the shame
of slavery.

Back to Via Dolorosa's hurly-burly,
I leave Esther safe with the Armenians;
they too understand what suffering is.

Maria Terrone | Erased

I   was 21.
I   was in my first post-college job.
I   had long, straight hair
        then, only then.

I   worked downtown when it was
        still seedy.
I   left the office at 5 p.m.
I   was on an empty street,
        heading home.

        It was summer.
        Summer was in   me.
        My new husband was in me.
I   would soon be home.

I   saw the man coming.

He   was lurching,
        reached out,
        grabbed hard between my legs.

        I shook.
        Alone on that street.
        Rooted in concrete.
Not   able to speak.
Not.
Not   I.
Just Not.
No,   that didn't happen.
Not   to me.
Not   me anymore.
Not   I.

Nil.
Nada.
No-   thing.

Maria Terrone | Exposed: A Publisher's Pathogens

Working in communications at the Manhattan headquarters of Avon Products, which proudly called itself "the woman's company," I never experienced sexism either overtly or subtly. I did experience all of the insanity for which the beauty industry is justifiably famous — constantly shifting goals, creative teams pitted against one another, the impeccably manicured claws of hyper-ambition drawing blood from anyone blocking its upward path.

When Avon share prices plunged and hundreds of middle managers, myself included, were laid off, I applied for a high-paying position at the largest book publisher in the United States. I applied despite the fact that I didn't want to be editor of its employee newspaper. In addition, I'd heard negative things about the CEO, who was widely known to be having an affair with one of the editors. I'd also been told that the vice president of Human Resources (I'll call him Mr. R), with whom I was soon scheduled to meet, was a man on the prowl. This warning had been shared by a friend, a management consultant who'd had contact with him a few years earlier at another company.

But what choice did I have? The economy was terrible and employment opportunities scarce.

After the usual interview questions from Mr. R, I was surprised to find myself being escorted by him to the office of the silver-haired CEO. Mr. R introduced me and then left. Mr. CEO had both feet up on his desk while he sipped a glass of wine — to celebrate his birthday, he said — inviting me to join him for a toast. He appeared jaded, world-weary, even a bit sad, and I politely declined the invitation. When the time came to review my editorial portfolio, he gestured to a large sofa where he sat uncomfortably close to me, his leg practically touching mine.

I'd worked at Avon and another Fortune 500 company, a community newspaper, and two Italian American magazines, but this was the first time I'd experienced what felt like predatory behavior, masked by feigned interest in my published clips. Before receiving an official job offer, I was asked to take on several freelance projects as a kind of test. One involved reporting on a business-related event for the company's employees, and it was then that Mr. R used the crowded room as an opportunity to "accidentally" brush my breast with his hand. He said nothing, as if it hadn't happened, and I said nothing but was unnerved.

When I was offered the position, I accepted, but from day one, I was filled with dread and loathing. The dreariness of that rainy first day on the job matched my mood. I soon learned that the preppy male administrative assistant assigned to me had a contemptuous air, and he seemed to take special pleasure in not delivering important phone messages. Was misogyny a job requirement or just part of the toxic atmosphere originating from the top floor? My direct supervisor had just been hired, too — a woman whose big-shouldered power suits, clipped directives, and success-at-any-cost style communicated her toughness.

I found myself working from 9 a.m. to 7:30 p.m. every day and then bringing more work home. About three weeks into the job, I developed a strange, debilitating illness marked by lingering fever. My doctor at the time just shook his head as I described my feeling of utter exhaustion. (I didn't tell him about my feeling of utter hopelessness.) From my sickbed, I received my supervisor's phone assignments, which I felt compelled to complete, writing pad and paper clips scattered in the sheets.

The morning of my return to work several weeks later, HR summoned me. A manager I'd never met explained that I couldn't expect to be accommodated with a 9-to-5 schedule, even temporarily (my doctor's request), because my position was just too demanding. I wonder now if this firing due to my sudden illness was legal, but at the time, I felt only huge relief and the lifting of a crushing weight from my body.

In Susan Sontag's 1978 work *Illness as Metaphor*, she argues against the idea that illness is an expression of the sufferer's character. By using metaphor to describe illness, she suggests, patients are shamed and silenced. "The most truthful way of regarding illness — and the healthiest way of being ill — is one most purified of, most resistant to, metaphoric thinking," she writes [Sontag, 1978, 3]. But I disagree. Among others who have refuted her thesis, physician/poet Jack Coulehan remarks on how Sontag overlooks the essential and positive ways we use metaphoric imaginings to cope and find meaning in our lives.

I'm certain that the publishing company's atmosphere was like poison seeping into me, or to use another metaphor, a pathogen infecting me, and my body and soul rebelled, shutting down like a drawbridge against invaders. Not long after I was let go, my symptoms disappeared, and I found an equally demanding — but happily fulfilling and meaningful — communications position at the university where I've made my career.

Resources: "Illness as Metaphor by Susan Sontag," annotated by Jack Coulehan, MD, MPH, NYU Langone Health LITMED Database, May 20, 1997. Sontag's book was published by Farrar, Straus, Giroux, New York.

Tina Tocco | A Newly Made Wife

These walls have kept
a newly made wife,
her good provider,

have witnessed three children into life.
Each room filled, tended by
a newly made wife

who was taught not to cry.
Forfeit all choice.
Each room filled, tended by

hands, thighs, a concrete inner voice.
That one refrain:
Forfeit all choice.

Her strength, she was taught, is best used to maintain
the secrets of
that one refrain.

And because she must stay for more than love,
these walls have kept
the secrets of
her good provider.

Camilla Trinchieri | *Anch'io* (#MeToo)

Anch'io, I tell myself now that so many women are confessing, accusing. I say it in Italian because the first time it happened I was a seven-year-old just sent by my American grandparents to live with my Italian father working in Austria. Instead of going to the American school, Papà puts me in a German-speaking school. Young children learn languages so quickly, he must have thought. The class for girls is full. I will learn with only boys. They turn out to be harmless, almost nonexistent. The teacher, a redhead, likes to call on me to read next to him. Hidden by his desk I struggle with the Gothic script while he slips his hand inside my panties and strokes me. I don't react, keep reading. This goes on for a whole semester. Later I develop a dislike for men with red hair, but it takes me years to put the two together. The teacher did not affect me in any deep way, or so I have believed all these years. The catechism priest I caught looking at pornographic pictures stopped my breath only a second or two. More instances back in Italy and here in the States — not interesting. I write this now, and a moment later, catch myself. How can I call "not interesting" a friend trying to rape me?

I have spoken of the incidents before to friends, in a calm, 'there it is' voice, the way one might speak about a missed school day or a cake that did not rise. I want to confess the incidents and write about them the way I always have. *It's just water off a duck's back. No harm done. Don't be surprised. That's the way they are. I know it. Don't you?*

But I must not. Now I have an opportunity to open the door to the bank vault inside me where I keep — what? — I'm not sure. Nor am I sure I want to see what is there. I put up barriers: *Am I showing off by writing this, by joining the movement? Has #MeToo become a badge almost to be proud of? Am I shouting, "Look at me"?*

No!

And yet, a niggling doubt remains within me. I cannot accuse these men. I cannot muster anger. To do so would give them importance. I cannot. Why not? Each illicit touch has been a confirmation of the need to build a moat. In that vault I must have stored pain, mistrust, fear of another betrayal. I realize a man's hand stroking a child's behind, grasping her woman's breasts, forcing her legs apart is denying that she is his equal, and by denying, betraying me. Betraying all women. I should be screaming. All I feel is immense sadness.

Acknowledgments

Amy Barone
"I Quit"

Kamikaze Dance
Finishing Line Press, 2015

"I Quit" first appeared in
Impolite Conversation.

"Nineteenth and Sansom,"
"Summer Haze"

We Became Summer
New York Quarterly Books,
2018

"Nineteenth and Sansom"
first appeared in *Philadelphia
Poets.*

Paola Corso
"Girl Talk"

*Once I Was Told the Air Was
Not for Breathing*
Parallel Press, 2012

Marisa Frasca
"Battledress,"
"Taking Leave," and
"Smelling the Fox"

*Wild Fennel: Poems and
Other Stories*
Bordighera Press, 2019

Maria Mazziotti Gillan
"In Our House Nobody Ever
Said"

LIPS #46/47
ed. Laura Boss, 2017

Honorable Mention,
Beyond Baroque 7th Annual
Poetry Contest,
Judge: Diane Wakoski, 2016

Maria Giura
"At Fifteen"
"Rockin' Eve"
"Mary"

What My Father Taught Me
Bordighera Press, 2018

"Mary" first appeared in
Italian Americana, Volume
XXXV No. 2 Summer 2017.

Roxanne Marie Hoffman
"Girls' Night Out"

Commissioned for *Rockin' the
Mic Against Rape*, Bowery
Poetry Club, New York City,
September 20, 2006.
Organized by Not in Our City,
a grassroots project of the
New York City Alliance
Against Sexual Assault.

Nina Carey Tassi
"Esther in Her Nakedness"

Light & Glory
Cherry Grove Collections,
2018

Maria Terrone
"Erased"

Cream City Review, 43.1
Spring/Summer 2019

About the Contributors

B. Amore is an artist and writer. Her books include *Journeys on the Wheel* (Bordighera Press, 2020), *An Italian American Odyssey: Lifeline — filo della vita: Through Ellis Island and Beyond* (Center for Migration Studies, 2006), *Invisible Odysseys: Art by Mexican Farmworkers in Vermont / Odiseas Invisibles: Arte de trabajadores mexicanos en Vermont* (Kokoro Press, 2010), *Carving Out a Dream* (Kokoro Press, 2008). Art and poetry reviews appear in *Sculpture*, *Art New England*, and various other journals. Her creative writing is found in *Italian Americana*; *VIA*; *Bridging the Waters: An International Bilingual Poetry Anthology* (Korean Expatriate Literature, 2013); *Speaking Memory: Oral Culture and Italians in America* (Palgrave Macmillan, 2009); *Daughters, Dads, and the Path through Grief* (Impact, 2015); *The Italian Americans: A History* (PBS, 2015); and *Delirious Naples: A Cultural History of the City of the Sun* (Fordham University Press, 2018).

Amy Barone spent five years as an Italian correspondent in Milan for *Women's Wear Daily* and *Advertising Age*. Her latest poetry collection, *We Became Summer*, was released by New York Quarterly Books in 2018. Other publications include two chapbooks *Kamikaze Dance* (Finishing Line Press, 2015) and *Views from the Driveway* (Foothills Publishing, 2008), as well as several fine literary magazines and anthologies, including *Café Review*, *Gradiva*, *Maintenant*, *Paterson Literary Review*, *Sensitive Skin*, and *Standpoint*. She's a longtime member of PEN America and an active participant in Brevitas, the online poetry community that celebrates short poems. A native of Bryn Mawr, Pennsylvania, Barone splits her time between New York City and Philadelphia.

Grace Cavalieri was appointed Maryland Poet Laureate in 2019. She's the author of over twenty collections of poetry, including her latest, *What the Psychic Said* (Goss Publications, 2020), *Other Voices, Other Lives* (Alan Squire Publishing, 2017), and the 8th annual Bordighera Poetry Prize-winning *Water on the Sun* (published with translation by Maria Enrico, 2007). Cavalieri's also written texts and lyrics for opera, television, and film, and has had 26 plays produced on American stages. She teaches poetry workshops at numerous colleges throughout the country. As producer and host of the syndicated radio show *The Poet and the Poem*, aired weekly on WPFW-FM (1977–1997), she presented more than 2,000 poets to the nation. She now offers this series to public radio from the Library of Congress via NPR satellite and Pacifica Radio, celebrating over 40 years on air. Cavalieri has received multiple awards, including the 2019 Anne Arundel County Arts Council Award for Literary Arts, the 2013 George Garrett Award for Outstanding Community Service in Literature from AWP, and the Poetry Committee of the Greater Washington, DC's first Merit Award for her contribution to Washington poetry in 1992.

Olivia Kate Cerrone is the author of *The Hunger Saint* (Bordighera Press, 2017), a historical novella about Italy's child miners. Her Pushcart Prize-nominated fiction won the Jack Dyer Prize from *Crab Orchard Review*, a *Mason's Road* Literary Award, and took first place in an *Italian Americana* literary contest. She's written for *Psychology Today, Publishers Weekly, The Rumpus, The Brooklyn Rail*, and *The Huffington Post*. She has received fellowships from the Hawthornden Castle International Retreat for Writers, Ragdale Foundation, VCCA, Vermont Studio Center, Hambidge Center for the Creative Arts and Science, and the National Endowment for the Arts.

Paola Corso is a literary activist and author of six books of poetry and fiction. Her most recent, *The Laundress Catches Her Breath* (Cavankerry Press, 2012), set in her native Pittsburgh where her Italian immigrant family worked in the steel mills, won the Tillie Olsen Award in Creative Writing. For *Once I Was Told the Air Was Not for Breathing* (University of Wisconsin–Madison, 2012), she was honored by the Triangle Fire Memorial Association in 2018. A New York Foundation on the Arts poetry fellow and Sherwood Anderson Fiction Award winner, Corso co-edited with Dr. Nandita Ghosh the anthology *Politics of Water: A Confluence of Women's Voices*, published by Routledge Press, 2007.

Donna DiCello, PsyD, is a clinical psychologist in private practice in New Haven, Connecticut, where she also works as an Assistant Clinical Professor at the Yale University School of Medicine. Her love of the written word has evolved into poems, many published in literary journals including *Bethlehem Writers Roundtable, Minerva Rising*, and *Blue Heron Review*. She co-authored with Lorraine Mangione *Daughters, Dads, and the Path through Grief: Tales from Italian America* (Impact, 2015), an exploration of father/daughter relationships and loss through the stories of fifty Italian American women.

Jessica Femiani, after graduating from Wesleyan University in Connecticut, moved to New York City where she first worked as a case manager with at-risk and homeless youth, and then as an English Teacher in Corona, Queens. Her poems and essays have been published in the *Paterson Literary Review*, and she has been a finalist for the journal's annual Allen Ginsberg Poetry Award. Femiani has read her poetry with the Italian American Writers Association and at the New York City Poetry Festival. She has also presented her work at the annual conferences of the Italian American Studies and Working Class Studies Associations. She now lives and works in Upstate New York, where she is pursuing a doctorate in English and creative writing at Binghamton University, SUNY.

Marisa Frasca is a bilingual poet, translator, book reviewer, and the author of *Wild Fennel: Poems and Other Stories* (Bordighera Press, 2019). Her work has been widely published in literary journals and anthologies, among them: *The Stillwater Review*; *Italian Americana*; *Veils, Halos & Shackles: International Poetry on the Oppression & Empowerment of Women* (Kasva Press LLC, 2016); *Embroidered Stories: Interpreting Women's Domestic Needlework from the Italian Diaspora* (University Press of Mississippi, 2015); and *The Journal of Italian Translation*. Frasca's more recent work is forthcoming in *Making Mirrors: Writing/Righting the Refugee Crisis* (Olive Branch Press, 2019) and *Kexaptùn: Poetry in NYC's Oldest and Newest Languages*, a project of the Endangered Language Alliance. Born in Vittoria, Italy, she currently resides on Long Island.

Maria Mazziotti Gillan, whose most recent publications include the poetry and photography collaboration with Mark Hillringhouse, *Paterson Light and Shadow* (Serving House Books, 2017), and *What Blooms in Winter* (New York Quarterly Books, 2016), is the author of twenty-two books. She received the American Book Award for *All that Lies Between Us* (Guernica Editions, 2009). Gillan is the Founder and Executive Director of the Poetry Center at Passaic County Community College in Paterson, New Jersey, Editor of the *Paterson Literary Review*, and Professor of Poetry and Director of the Creative Writing Program at Binghamton University, SUNY.

Daniela Gioseffi is an American Book Award-winning author of 17 books of poetry and prose. She's published in *The Nation, The Paris Review, Prairie Schooner, Poetry International, Rain Taxi Review,* and *Chelsea Literary Review*; in anthologies from HarperCollins, Viking, Penguin Books, and Oxford University Press. The first of her seven collections of poetry is *Eggs in the Lake* (BOA Editions, 1979), and her latest is *Waging Beauty: As the Polar Bear Dreams of Ice* (Poets Wear Prada, 2017). She's won NYSCA/NEA grant awards and a John Ciardi Award for Lifetime Achievement in Poetry. Her verse appears etched in marble on a wall of New York Penn Station, along with Walt Whitman's. She's presented poems on WNYC, NPR, and BBC, on campuses throughout the USA and Europe, and at international book fairs from Barcelona to Miami. She is Editor-in-Chief of Eco-Poetry.org, an online archive dedicated to climate crisis concerns, receiving six thousand global visitors monthly.

Maria Giura's latest book, *Celibate: A Memoir,* was published by Apprentice House in 2019. Her work, which has appeared in various literary journals, including *Prime Number, Presence, Lips, Italian Americana,* and *VIA,* has garnered awards from the Academy of American Poets, the *Paterson Literary Review,* and Salem College's Center for Women Writers. She was also a finalist for the Milton Center Fellowship and a judge for the Lauria/Frasca Poetry Prize. Giura has taught literature and writing at St. John's University, Montclair State University, and Binghamton University, SUNY, where she received her PhD.

Roxanne Marie Hoffman earned her MPhil from NYU's Stern School of Business, worked for twenty years at JPMorgan Chase, and was an active member of the New York Chapter of ACM's Special Interest Group Woman in Banking in the eighties. Over a hundred of her spoken word recordings and poems have appeared online and in print. Her publication credits include the IndieFeed: Performance Poetry online archive, *Pedestal Magazine*, *Hospital Drive*, *So It Goes: The Literary Journal of the Kurt Vonnegut Memorial Library*, *The Bandana Republic: A Literary Anthology by Gang Members and Their Affiliates* (Soft Skull Press, 2008), *From the Porch Swing: Memories of Our Grandparents* (Silver Boomer Books, 2010), and *The Waiting Room Reader* (CavanKerry Press, 2013). She and Jack Cooper run Poets Wear Prada, an independent literary press that has published Rosalie Calabrese, Daniela Gioseffi, and Maria Lisella, among many others.

Maria Lisella is the sixth Queens Poet Laureate and curates the Italian American Writers Association reading series in New York. Her Pushcart Prize-nominated work appears in her three poetry collections, *Thieves in the Family* (New York Quarterly Books, 2014), *Amore on Hope Street* (Finishing Line Press, 2009), and *Two Naked Feet* (Poets Wear Prada, 2009). Her poetry also appears in several anthologies including *The Traveler's Vade Mecum* (Red Hen Press, 2017). Lisella also writes essays and short stories, and these have been included in *What Does it Mean to be White in America?* (2LeafPress, 2016), *She Can Find Her Way* (Upper Hand Press, 2017), and *A Feast of Narrative* (IdeaPress, 2020). By day she is Europe Editor for *Travel Market Report* and a frequent contributor to *USA Today*, *The Jerusalem Post*, and *La Voce di New York*.

Lorraine Mangione, PhD, teaches in the Department of Clinical Psychology at Antioch University New England. Much of her writing, research, and practice centers around women, including a recent academic article with Donna Luff on the female fans of Bruce Springsteen [*Bruce Springsteen and Popular Music Rhetoric, Social Consciousness, and Contemporary Culture*. ed. William I.

Wolff, London: Routledge, 2017, Chapter 8: "Who is Springsteen to his women fans?"] and another with Rosalind Forti on women, aging, and group therapy [*International Journal of Group Psychotherapy*, Volume 68, 2018 - Issue 3, "Beyond Midlife and Before Retirement: A Short-Term Women's Group," pp. 314-336]. She co-authored with Donna DiCello *Daughters, Dads, and the Path through Grief: Tales from Italian America* (Impact, 2015), an exploration of father/daughter relationships and loss through the stories of fifty Italian American women.

Joanne Monte is a poet and novelist. Her poems have appeared in literary journals, such as *Poet Lore, The Raintown Review,* and *Twilight Ending,* and have merited her recognition, most notably, a John David Johnson Memorial Poetry Award (First Place, 1998) and Honorable Mentions from Writer's Digest and New Millennium, both in 1999. In 2012 she received the Bordighera Poetry Prize for *The Blue Light of Dawn,* a collection of poems encompassing human rights issues. Her novel set during the Korean War, *The Day to Eternity* (Word Association, 2012), has been favorably reviewed, described as a "gripping narrative" and a "highly informative novel." She also serves on the editorial and advisory board for Eco-Poetry.org, a website dedicated to promoting public awareness of the repercussions of climate change.

Kathryn Nocerino is a native New Yorker with a fine arts background who writes in multiple genres. New Rivers Press published two poetry books: *Wax Lips* (1996) and *Death of the Plankton Bar & Grill* (1996); Warthog Press brought out a third, *Candles in the Daytime* (1985). Among the anthologies which include her work are *Growing up Ethnic in America* and *Identity Lessons: Contemporary Writing About Learning to Be American,* both released by Penguin Books in 1999, and edited by Maria Mazziotti Gillan and Jennifer Gillan.

Angelina Oberdan is a writer and instructor from Charlotte, North Carolina. She received an MFA in creative writing from McNeese State University in Lake Charles, Louisiana. Angelina's work has appeared in many journals, including *Cold Mountain Review, Italian Americana, Möbius, Southern Indiana Review,* and *Yemassee.* She co-edited a collection of essays by and about Daniela Gioseffi, *Pioneering Italian American Culture: Escaping La Vita Della Cucina* (Bordighera Press, 2013), and wrote the introduction to *Guest in the Woods* (Chelsea Press, 2013), a bilingual collection of poetry by Elisa Bagiani.

Lisa Marie Paolucci is a doctoral candidate in English Education at Teachers College, Columbia University. She serves as the assessment coordinator of the Education Department at St. Francis College where she is also an adjunct lecturer. After earning her Master of Arts in English from Brooklyn College, where she studied Italian American literature, she served as a member of the Executive Council of the Italian American Studies Association and on the Board of the Italian American Writers Association. Paolucci co-wrote the libretto for the opera short *Little Orphant Annie,* which was produced by the Remarkable Theater Brigade at Carnegie Hall in 2011.

Michelle Reale is a professor at Arcadia University and a doctoral candidate in Educational Leadership. She holds an MFA in poetry. She is the author of eleven books of poetry, including her latest, *Season of Subtraction* (Bordighera Press, 2019), and the forthcoming *Confini: Poems of Refugees in Sicily* (Červená Barva Press, 2020) and *In the Blink of a Mottled Eye* (Kelsay Books, 2020). She is the founding and managing editor of *Ovunque Siamo: New Italian American Writing.* She has been twice nominated for a Pushcart prize

Nina Carey Tassi is a resident of New York City and holds a PhD in English from Fordham University. She has worked as a college teacher and university administrator in both Maryland and New York. Her published books of poetry include *The Jeremiah Tree* (Blurb, 2011) with fine art by Jeanine Rivard Malaney, *Antarctic Visions* (Xlibris, 2011) with photos by Pat Roach, *Spirit Ascending* (WordTech Communications LLC, 2016), and her most recent collection, *Light & Glory* (Cherry Grove Collections, 2018).

Maria Terrone is the author of three full-length poetry collections, *Eye to Eye* (Bordighera Press), *A Secret Room in Fall* (McGovern Prize, Ashland Poetry Press), and *The Bodies We Were Loaned* (The Word Works). Finishing Line Press published a chapbook, *American Gothic, Take 2*. Her work, which has been translated into French and Farsi and nominated five times for a Pushcart Prize, has appeared in more than 25 anthologies and various literary journals, including *Poetry*, *Ploughshares*, and *The Hudson Review*. Her first book of creative nonfiction, *At Home in the New World* (Bordighera Press), was published in 2018.

Tina Tocco's work has appeared in *Italian Americana, VIA, Roanoke Review, River Styx, Crab Creek Review, Harpur Palate, Passages North, Potomac Review, Portland Review*, and the anthology *Wild Dreams: The Best of Italian Americana* (Fordham University Press, 2008), among other publications. Tocco was a finalist in CALYX Press's 2013 Flash Fiction Contest and was awarded Honorable Mention in the *River Styx* 2015 Schlafly Beer Micro-Brew Micro-Fiction Contest. Her interview on flash and the craft of writing, "No Wasted Words," was published in *Roanoke Review*. Tocco earned her MFA in creative writing from Manhattanville College, where she served as editor-in-chief for *Inkwell*.

Camilla Trinchieri worked for many years dubbing films in Rome. She immigrated to the USA in 1980 and received an MFA in creative writing from Columbia University. Under the pseudonym Camilla T. Crespi, she has published seven Simona Griffo Mysteries with HarperCollins. *The Breakfast Club Murder* was published by Five Star in 2014. As Camilla Trinchieri, she has published *The Price of Silence* (Soho Press, 2007) and *Seeking Alice* (SUNY Press, 2016), a fictionalized account of her mother's life in Europe during WWII, which won an Italian American Studies Association award. Both have been translated and published in Italy.

A NOTE ON THE TYPE

Text here is set in Constantia, a serif font designed by John Hudson. One of six typefaces commissioned by Microsoft for extended on-screen reading (and the initial letter "C"), Constantia, released in 2006, takes its name from Latin, meaning "constancy." And as its name might suggest, works well both in print and on screen. Anne Van Wagener, reviewing Microsoft's new ClearType Font Collection in 2005 for *Poynteronline*, a zine for journalists, writes:

> Constantia is my favorite [of the suite]. It's really a beautiful typeface that is very clean and readable. The italic isn't fussy and the numerals are strong and sophisticated. . . . Created for use in print or on the screen, its versatility would enable a publication to use it for both print and Web operations. It creates a consistent look or brand in both mediums.

At odds with company lawyers whose fear of trademark infringement continued to narrow the choices of possible nomenclature, Hudson, one evening, singing psalms during vespers, heard "constantia" intoned. He later confessed that the sight of seabirds had made him regret that he hadn't chosen to call the typeface Cormorant.

The Design Desk, "The Next Big Thing in Online Type," March 4, 2005, www.poynter.org